CONTENTS

M000034795

PART ONE

PART TWO

CAPE COAST CASTLE

KWADWO OPOKU-AGYEMANG

AFRAM PUBLICATIONS (GHANA) LIMITED

Published by
Afram Publications (Ghana) Ltd.
P. O. Box M.18
Accra, Ghana.

First Published, 1996

ISBN 9964 70 170 5

Typeset by
Damana Graphics

Printed and bound by
The Advent Press, P.O. Box 0102,
Osu-Accra, Ghana

PART THREE

The Meaning of Cape Coast Castle

Cape Coast Castle, the edifice and the metaphor, stands outside the limits of time. Its meaning is deliquescent. Its world is the world before naming, form or kinship. Knotty, full of discrepancies and confused codes, it rules by silence. The power of Cape Coast Castle is the power of silence, silence as the seduction and betrayal of power.

Any self-naming must resurrect memory and render past and present experience meaningful. It must betray silence. Even if it occurs in a burst of hysteria, such self-naming becomes a self-collecting, power gained over the scattered and the buried. To name Cape Coast Castle properly, therefore, means to grasp the full range and significance of the single most traumatic body of experience in all our known history.

Slavery is the living wound under the patchwork of scars. A lot of time has passed, yet whole nations cry, sometimes softly, sometimes harshly, often without knowing why. Listen to what the poet says: the same griefs flow down the stream; vast lands choke with weed; the people waste away. The slave trade persists in its effects: pain without form, drilling, alone, without kin; thus the persistence of the lament even in our happiest love-song; love, the common Akan saying goes, is death.

The voices within Cape Coast Castle are full of the scarring. The wound is real, the judgment of chaos is real. The various personnae who are engaged in the struggle will suffer, too, that starvation of the womb until Cape Coast Castle takes its true form.

The Grossle Bastion

The history of Cape Coast Castle begins simply enough. In 1650 a European who has come down to us in history simply as Crispe received permission from the king of Fetu, whose title was Dey, to build a fort on a promontory on the coast of Fanti-land. The country surrounding the stony cape was called Fetu, but the Portuguese named it Carbo Corco, Short Cape. Carbo Corco was later to be bastardized into the incongruent Cape Coast to make it more familiar to English ears. Crispe paid sixty pound sterling in goods for the piece of rock and it is reported that the people of Fetu jubilated over the sale. That same year the king of Fetu sold the same piece of land to a Pole in the employ of the Swedish African Company, a fledgling trading outfit. The Polish trader was called Henry Caerlof. He established the first fort on the site where today Cape Coast Castle stands. The Swedes called the fort Carolusburg for Charles X.

Cape Coast Castle is one of three slave castles on the coast of Ghana. The others are Elmina Castle and Christiansborg Castle. In all there are more than six dozen castles, forts and various trading posts on a coast-line of less than 500 kilometres. When the slave trade was abolished in 1848 there were counted seventy-six forts and castles of various sizes from Keta on the eastern coast to Half Assini on the Western seaboard. This gives Ghana what may very well be the highest concentration of slave-posts anywhere in the world. This crowded coastal stretch has been called the shopping street of West Africa. Among other commodities, the "shops" bought and sold Africans. Cape Coast Castle was not the first slave-shop. The dubious honour most probably belongs to the fort at Cromantine, built in 1640. However, Cape Coast Castle was the most important castle in the Slave Trade for the reason that at the height of the trade in Africans it served as the headquarters of the busiest European slave traders on the coast of present-day Ghana, the English.

The slave-dungeons in Cape Coast Castle emphasized the cruelty of the trade. In the 1680s when Greenhill's Point was added to the northern section of the castle, another new building, to the south and directly facing the sea, was constructed. This addition was roughly triangular; it formed a parade in whose enclosed space European troops probably regularly assembled for inspection and display. The parade stood above some large vaults whose sides where ventilated by grates. These vaults, mysterious underground holds, cramped, cavernous, dark, musty and airless, could contain over a thousand captives at any one time as they awaited the Middle Passage. Many died from lack of air. The airless darkness within the dungeons is the metaphor of a modern predicament whose vehicle is trauma.

In the 1790s the Dazel Towers were added. These were round, spacious and comfortable rooms that served as the governor's apartments. Deep down and directly underneath them was the Grossle Bastion; it, too housed slave dungeons in its time. The enslaved who found themselves unwilling occupants of these chtonic holes came mostly from the hinterlands. From such as these, blood and body abandoned to unknown agonies, came the African Diaspora.

These were the enslaved Africans, a people fired a deep bronze in the crucible, swept snarling through burning oceans and heated marshlands to the edge where cotton was king and cane sap sweetened the soil. Even bent under foreign skies the African in them came out, like dark spots on the sun. A weak people never built a world power, and we know

3

today that it was their sweat made fertile the soil of the New World. They gave us the gift of song and humanized the world they founded by vesting the meaning of freedom with a new density.

But what of the land and the survivors they left behind, the places and the people so savaged? The history of Africa in the four centuries of European slave trading is a history of internecine warfare and wanton destruction. The darkness of the dark continent was born here in the fretful culture of dense fear: "Something startles where I thought I was safest," wrote the poet, and his insight applies profoundly to the victims of the empire of darkness slavery made in Africa. One by one the light of learning and of life was dimmed, then was turned off. Thus began an eclipse whose effect we are still living. It is not remarked too often, but it is not for nothing that the collapse of the last of the great African civilizations coincided with the coming of the slave trade. From here on, for long centuries, scientific knowledge hid its head in the folds of magic and it died there from lack of air, from the fear to openly observe and testify to the fact and glory of life. Gibberish replaced the wise and healing word, and men talked more to gods than to each other. Out of sheer fear the industry of growth became the invention of gods and protective amulets. There is no point in denying the fact: the place so savaged becomes a place of savages; it becomes the victim society.

The Victim of Society: Graves Without Bodies

The basis of the history of a society can be defined in terms of the production and reproduction of immediate life. Production concerns the ways by which the means of subsistence, that is food, clothing, shelter and tools, are achieved. By reproduction we refer to a population replacing itself. When we speak of a victim society in the European slave trade, we mean the African land and its people from which were drained the captives of the trade. It is a victim society because its production and reproduction of immediate life, that is the basic sources of its life culture and history, were violently and irrevocably disrupted by the predatory European Society. The victim society is described as such because it was made to suffer a massive loss of its population; in addition its productive possibilities were ravaged and ransacked. Both its population growth and material growth came under great disruptive pressure.

The victim society consisted of the ordinary members of the community, neither slaving chief nor warlord, who were the object of capture. It also included the people who were given as gifts to slavers, or were haggled over and sold: captives, prisoners of war, the kidnapped and the total range of people swept away, or who daily suffered the threat of capture. Apart from the actual captives there were those killed in slave wars, and those who could not survive the arduous march to the castle.

Yet, tragic as the fate of all these victims is, perhaps the most horrendous experience of the victim society belonged to a group hardly ever mentioned in the literature: the damned who survived, those deprived relatives of the captured African. These included parents, brothers and sisters, uncles

5

and other relatives and friends who knew and cared for the captive. In a way, theirs was a lot *de profundis,* a loss of deepest death. For, they were denied the cathartic benefit of a burial for the loved ones. Olaudah Equiano, the 18th century African abolitionist, tells the story in his autobiography of 1789 of how, as a greening youth, he and his sister were kidnapped from their Igbo village by slavers while their parents were at their farm; brother and sister were sold into slavery, never to be seen ever again by their people. We know Equiano's story because he survived to write his life-story; and the history he reflects upon is the full story of Africa abroad, the history of the African Diaspora in miniature. As an early example of the Slave Narrative Equiano's autobiography provides a full view of the agony of enslavement lived from within. We are able to follow the details of Equiano's life and so can discover the intimate geography of his tribulations. His story becomes our story because we possess the text, the materia critica. And yet what we read is not the full story, only a portion of it. For, Equiano's mother came home from the farm one evening to find her only daughter and youngest son stolen, never to be heard from again. We do not know her story. Nobody knows the story of her grief.

The captured Africans left behind them graves without bodies in the collective memory of surviving kinsfolk. This remains one of the most enduring, oppressive and difficult legacies of the European slave trade in Africa: a gaping spread of pain wounding and widening and deepening the suffering of the victim society through the process of time-binding.

To discover a measure, one small teasing inkling, of the impact of slavery and the slave trade on African societies we shall have to think of Equiano's mother, her pain and suffering at the sudden and irrevocable loss of her children, the

6

uncertainty and wild fears she carries all her life-long years. We shall have to consider the measures she takes, orphaned-mother, and the adjustments she will make to her life, to her family, and to her society. And then we shall have to take this bundle of untamed agonies and multiply it not by one woman, not by one family, not by one fearful village but by a continentful of people, living hearts of unspoken fear. We shall have to consider what such precarious living does to motherhood, fatherhood, attitudes to child rearing, community organization, education, the arts, religion, science, medicine, the very ontological basis of society. This is merely a way to enter Africa's culture under siege.

The World does not listen to Silence

A society that lives under a real and constant threat of enslavement consists of potential slaves, and a society of potential slaves will experience a cultural and psychological development peculiar to its environment. With the danger of capture constant, certain innate biologically-determined drives to self-preservation will develop. The culture will acquire certain characteristics and tendencies in order to adapt to and survive the danger. It may, for example, assume a posture of perpetual defensiveness. A highly developed sense of survival may help a society to endure the roving malignancy, but that instinct may become an impediment to growth when life itself may not reach beyond shrill survival. When a society is thus pitched and cannot do more than preserve its collective life, then its culture will fold into itself: it becomes a grim and conservative society, the people huddle together, furtive, subsisting by cunning, afraid even of the tremor lurking in the light.

7

The society that endures this age of trauma would become pathogenic, its environment contaminated. Except if critically examined with a view to healing it, the disease would be passed from generation to generation. Remnants of attitudes, relationships, views, ideals, morals and traditions from the enslaved society would persist through the ages. Thus, although ostensibly freed from the chains of enslavement and the curse of Cape Coast Castle, the germs of the disease would remain, hidden even in the walls of present joy and freedoms to waste efforts away. And in the absence of evidence of physical pathology, we would all wonder why a people should suffer so.

But, when it is forgotten or its lessons are ignored, history has a way of erupting or, with calculated cruelty (as if it had a mind all of its own), it visits in driblets until it forms a slow flood and sweeps everything away in a sea of madness. The effects of enslavement have lasted this long because of the silence that surrounds its history. The Mandingos say: "one adds to the power of the fetish by leaving it in the bag". The power of the fetish of slavery is enhanced by keeping it hidden. Growing out of the rock upon which it stands, Cape Coast Castle today is a blind permanence, the white-heat center of a pyre, anguish become a castle, a castle as a sign both of the triumph of others over us and of our seemingly rootless grief: rootless because we are so silent. But the world does not listen to silence.

The Castle has to be seen as a threat and a humiliation, a living and active reminder of this society as victim: how it began, why it began, why it has to go and how it has to go. The Castle is a standing provocation to thought and action: upon its disarming rests a whole people's freedom. Cape Coast Castle, the metaphor and the edifice, is a society in itself, a society of

8

experiences, a system or order whose fundamental concepts are planted in the disordering of our society. We kneel because it stands, and it stands for a system of production, distribution and exchange. But it does not tend what it produces, does not nurture what it distributes, does not value what it exchanges. There is no tending, no nurturing, no valuing. Cape Coast Castle achieves what it values by uprooting what it does not grow, by seeking to destroy a people and make of them a victim society.

The fact is that the pressures of our societies today, the tributes we pay in blood - colonialism, neo-colonialism, even poverty and the lopsided world order - are largely the effects of the slave trade. In the trade, societies were ransacked, the land was gutted, its human loam was washed to the sea, its potential was stunted. The people turned in arrested, some by greed, others by fear and uncertainty. However unpleasant it may be, the direst wishes of the enslaving racist scholars became true, not because Africans are created inferior or any such nonsense but because of the concrete historical experience of slavery itself. Slavery gives the enslaved nothing but a legacy of pain, alienation, fear, and worst of all, a fetish erected around the denial of the fact and lasting effects of enslavement. It is a fetish that allows us to pretend that our world is whole; thus we nullify the castle by incorporating, then ignoring it. The pretence, so well sustained, becomes reality. And so we live in a shattered world with an eroded sense of history in a world we swear is whole. Jolts, breaks and gasps are our calm. The common moments that take us everyday to the edge - crucial, radical, immediate and fearful - are lived as normal, and thus we genuflect in our daily grind under the power of the castle. To dissolve the fetish it is necessary to keep the story of slavery and the slave trade open-ended and to avoid closure; to clear the way to debate and to perpetually initiate rather than conclude the argument so that every new generation may visit it to quarry its lessons.

Uncertain as are the lives and gait of *Cape Coast Castle*, the poem, we are compelled to a new orientation simply by breaking the ancient silence. Naming the trauma involves exploring the condition of our daily world, past, present and future, and our work and promise that lie in it.

FOUR HUNDRED YEARS OF
ETERNAL VIGILANCE

PART I

CAPE COAST CASTLE

Introit

[handwritten: → biblical parallel]

AND THE SEA cackled, foaming at the mouth
Till dry cracks ploughed the waves back;
Hope, said the sea, is not a method
There are too many sad stories
Carved in indifferent stones:

There is always another story
After this is told
And words after the words
Of this world:
Did our elders not say
The boats leave but the people stay?

Behind the dawn stand
Queues of days, nibbles at debts
The lonely poor dropping from sight

Behind the dawn, nothing
Save the bones of sad stories:
History does not repeat itself
It merely quotes us
When we have not been too wise

The Watch

WAITING AT the beach awash with pride
To welcome back every running tide
That throws itself at my feet;
Waiting to worry back
Every turning wind
That would scatter my word;
Waiting, will till freed
And my mouth cleared of all weed

Every incoming wave is my witness
Every fishing seagull's cry is a guess
Every scattered grain of sand
A reason to replant this land

Too many sad stories are lost to stain
In the castle's cracks and leaning turrets
Too long have I stood silenced in the shadows
Where people got carried away by the bargain
I am waiting, will till freed
And our memory cleared of weed

Of Ghosts and Guests

I FUCKED with the law
And I travelled the twisted road by night
The brash jingles shadowed me
Calling me to the new jungle
Calling me home to the house of slaves
Hear me: I was dipped into song at birth
I know what paths lead to the curve in the moon
And what royalty squats on the throne
In the house of slaves

And it came to pass, the slave ship,
Bearing a new god
It crossed the path and the stream
It pacified proverbs
And their argument of who is elder
And that is the whole matter

disrespects ancient traditions

Let us then hear the conclusion of the matter
I am cousin to the rock upon which the castle stands
I fucked with the law when I refused to cross myself
I travelled down the cantankerous road
And I heard the sweet siren of the dying
The ghosts and their guests clearing their throat
I have been to the dungeons to feed the ghosts;
Was I scared? I fear more the silence of the living

15

In the Shadow of the Castle

WHERE TODAY sellers get carried away
By the bargain
Our people who are no longer of us
Also pleaded and waited fearfully
For the truth of betrayal:
They too got carried away

I have felt my way
And bent down low
I have touched seed
O gods, let me live, freed

Howl the Waking Deep

YET WHAT thoughts kept them company
Kept mind cocooned
Breath-held against such infinitude?
What strength carried them
Down the hollow wailing deep
Into the gut-rot: there to die
Die again, be witness to unending death?
What future lay waiting, poised to pounce
Hidden in the moist corners?

Oh howl the waking deep
The chained bloody investiture
Wrinkled round mourning;
Howl the furious dying

The palms writhen ululating
Howl the vivid hope playing the assassin's song

The faces that cling to us
Are of places far and plenty
And are of plenty with gleeful grace
For the night is stark
We walk among the towering faceless
And direst wishes follow the path of sale
Howl the wail bursting tight with blood
Blazing hands, dagger without end
Howl the fleshless sleep, the spiked dream
The chest full with sordid gold
Howl the castle
Church big enough for God   -
Howl the carriers of the cross
Hunchbacked by leaden piety
And howl too the shipwrecked hand of God

The Executioner's Dance

AND THE sea mourns under us
Because it remembers the dead
And the widowed rivers that fed it

But no one knows the castle now
No one cares. Forgotten,
It sits blending by fading
And by ruining
Keeps a low profile

The careful coast pinned its future
To the fat ships' cargoes
And threw the rest to the sharks
The vultures of the sea
Our pain, no longer youthful
Steps with care
Among the rubbled gates;
Without reason without care
All we hope for
Is going home to a curled rest

Blood broke the ground
Made the spirit damp
Made bracken the stools of chiefs
Thus the sun went round and round
Like a mad man looking for his head
And the shepherd of souls
Threw the hoes and the enslaved in the shed

I thought of peace
And the wish cut my tongue.
Our pain, no longer muffled

Steps with a yelp
Among the bones of history
And it does the executioner's dance
In the dungeons of the castle

And anger hot and rude
Enters without knocking

March of the Chain-Gang

HE IS riven
Twelve years of water:
Hasn't felt yet
The stirring of virgin erection

Come evening
He listens awed
To the stories of the brown earth
When sleep returns muddy
From the gossiping bush

They gripped his virginity
In an old vise
Plucked out his baby's courage;
Unacquainted with bribery
Or suicides s cold leer
He weighed clear-eyed
The dying promise

And the castle watched,
Fat as God

Sengbe Pieh *

HE SMELT THE dry season before it came

Moved like a maroon
Dealt rhythm like a hoofer
A wispy chest of wind
Bending rocks
Dusk chained by the neck
To dawn

Mayagilalo danced without music
Like a wizard

At sea Sengbe Pieh lived in the sanctuary of his skull
The storm stole his voice
He gave nothing away

Thus he searched everywhere
Looking for freedom in everything
He found it on deck in a spike

Those who perished in the sea perished
Trailed like a retort
To charity into a new order
Where large chaoses savaged the jungle's answer

Ruiz and Montez went like thieves into the blight
Ruiz, Montez and Celestino, queer little angel:
O my mountain lion
My gods become echo

*   *Sengbe Pieh : In 1839 on board the Spanish slave boat Amistad, he led a
    successful overthrow of the slavers and ordered the captain to sail into
    the sun, back to Africa.*

21

The storm stole my voice
I gave nothing away
Listen: the path struggles, and somehow
Overcomes the hill
And the season's take a reasoned course

He sneaked on the sun, Sengbe Pieh
Turned east against west in the sunset
Sengbe Pieh returned as sea
His hair misted with white and danger;
Foaming at the mouth as the sea
. A white kiss on the horizon

Equiano *

THE RAIN fell with craft and care
Insinuated itself on rooftops
Then made welcome by spreading passages
Haunted the resolve out of the gutters

The night came and went
And the day was sad to be back
What living reason
But to stay dead?

In the common turn
Of every season
The castle's kingdom stood
A buried inability:

Night ganged against dawn
The land leaked into the sea
No sadder feet moved the sands

The days lurched forward
Grappling with unbottled devils:
This one is Equiano, twelve
No statute of limitation
No crime against humanity
The castle is kind

---

* *Olaudah Equiano aka Gustavus Vassa : Born 1745 east of Niger River,
captured by slave raiders at age ten and sold into slavery. Bought his
freedom for 40 pounds sterling and worked in the anti-slavery movement.
In 1789 published his autobiography.*

The Slave Ship
(Equiano's Travels Chapter Three)

A DAY bombed out of its mind
Without pride without lust
Or knowledge of its immortality
A day of clay when all our eternity
Will dry up behind us, and before us
Vast deserts of death and another day

The rain will fall to its knees
(An aura of poisoned patter)
And the soil, receding,
Be settled and unsettling

What peace there is
Will multiply the barren wars

The clouds will flee
The outskirts of the sky
To die among the bones of great rivers
Here is fragile flesh, broken breath
Brutalized yolk, soothing lies
Old hills bleeding at their roots
And people too drunk to cry halt

The trees will raise their legs
And the world, our world
Will hang from the commonest branch

Supplication:
Equiano's Mother

I

Pain ripe beyond bearing
Settle rush seed in her lap

She lived with animal pain:
The nails of Christ
Shriek pierce her naked side
Pain as supple shadows in the deep

Pain so bold it sits there in clay to dry
The way to the shrine is a river of blood
Sometimes doing nothing
She'd shiver in her shrunken torment
And draw blood slicing snails

Sometimes sitting by the wayside
Breaking nuts with the rats
And the crabs that know enough
To walk sideways from hillocks of skulls
She'd see to the clear bottom of torment
Anguish squared in cornered eyes

II

She shouts her own name to the passing wind
That something in time will remember her proper name
The rush seed, the animal pain and the cornered eyes
At the shrine where skulls parade the Apirede dance
Child of the crocodile, she is beating water
Chasing the dead with her dirge.

III

Then she untied the two pieces of kola
And placed them deep in the well of closest desire
The woman who birthed both mother and child prayed:
·Flesh of my flesh, grandchild of the leopard
The woman who is father to all children
This is blood, the red blood of kin
This is the gourd of charms
The whisk from the cave in the rock
I ask you: why do they not return
Those who go?

I have covered myself with earth
I have touched the bitter weed to my tongue
And my stone has worn down the axe
I have travelled to the place
Where God first drew fire
Where the wild boar got drunk
The bond between lines, where is it today?
Take me to the outskirts of the town
And leave me there alone with the vultures
Leave me to stumble among the skulls
Among the jawbones that even in death smile at God
I have something hard to say
Hold me, hold me down
I fear to report the endless death
No place is safe, not even my own mouth
And the words that lie in it, how true are they
To the few who hear?

Equiano's Retort

THE PEOPLE looked up
The stars were salt; beneath them
The earth had fled, making no sound

Our earth ascended the horizon
Blood was like ash
They caught the frenzy and opened fire
Blood called as voice and its echo
And nobody heard our dying call.
At dawn the raiders came
The men and the women were at the farm
The raiders knocked down the doors
They scattered the ash and the old people
They killed the young in their yolk
They spread anguish on rooftops
The winds came down from the mountains
Dragging along the foul air from the smoking ruins

Everything is present in my memory
Even the far future, the buried fury

In silence and alone
Mothers hear the cries of their stolen children
The castle breathes sweetness
Who will protect you from your history
Read to your children the book of conquest?

importance of memory

In silence and alone
Fathers swallow their clenched fist
Now they are mute on the road of thorns
And the clouds have eaten the moon:

If people died of all the things they remember
We would live forever.

27

The Loneliness of the Sea

THE NIGHT of our hour of capture
The whip branded the time wounded
Thus hard by the sea we shared
The loneliness of the sea

Out of the spray sprang two strangers
One was crab-like, me
He stood still, and thus rocked
With the loneliness of the sea

The other knew the lie of the land
Knew enough not to explain the sun's heat
The reasons men stand aloft
In the deep solitude of the sea

Both were caught in common glow
Men who rose and fell with the sea
In time made chaste
By the loneliness of the sea

We knew the flat meandering of the sea
The destitution of quick answers
The hobbled land straining to wayward song
The deep draining into the lonely sea

We came as none will after us
And left to them alone
Still will be in the days left to us
And the welling loneliness of the sea

Thus must we remember if only to test
The castle's hunger
The captive eyes swirling in their heads

Like fallen leaves in the wind
A history only of forgotten memories
Chips, bits, cracks and carapace
And our earth's cry beyond the loneliness of the sea

Elmina has no Twilight

ELMINA HAS no twilight
No blight, no past in sight
The past is now, it smells
Of kerosene, rotten fish in barrels

And the palm trees shake their head
Disagreeing as usual with wind and sea

The castle stands on a hillock
History on tiptoe:
The races speak to each other
Of the drama of the sea in the sand

turbulence still [handwritten margin note]

El Mina, 1498 *

IT WAS A DARK COMING

IT WAS a dark coming
The day entered sideways
And night was narrow, full of tunnels

They draped my native
In crossbones and blight
And turning in the wind
Drove down the peril with the nail

Painted a blotched white on my ire
Ill-favoured, sea and canticle

It was a dark coming
Dark as white over glacier eyes
And they set up shop on the shore
Cannon and turret
Ball and chain
A twist of lime in bile, with chasers:

Sat a chapel on my temple)

Cracked! They cracked!
From wine, dirt, sex and cant
Governor and chieftain embraced
Sent menace up-country
All surfaces gritty, pouched and seamy
Musty walls green with infertile grime)   Smells of
A smell of death invading)   dungeons

* *El Mina, 1498 : Year of Portuguese arrival in Edina, in the Gold Coast.* ·

31

Thus the mist stays, sold blood irks
And the past lives on in the mind
Beyond the whitewash, beyond the babble
Somehow the mind survives the past
And the bareness of memory

It was a dark coming
The severance, the evacuated pregnancy
The invading smell of death:
The sea saw them all
But unable to talk
Today mumbles and roars by turn
And the wind still turns in the chill

It was a dark dark turning
The day entered askew
And night was tight, full of tumbles

Contrasts
beginning

Cape Coast Town

YOU CAN tell
By the way it leans
Exhausted
The erect ambitions
It has weathered

My life flows seaward
A slow day-dream dissolving
With the irrational streets
The back-handed charm
The night-mud houses
Their eyes half-shut

An aged town
It stands on the one good foot
Shaking and forgetful

everlasting pain

What matters
Is not just the ruins
Or the years devouring one another
But the veins
That still escape with the blood

33

Pacotille *

TAKE IT or leave it
A deal is a deal:

13 beads of coral
$1/2$ a string of amber
28 silver bells
3 pairs of bracelets

And here
For your favourite wife
Some rows of glassbeads
And, Ah! (but I am too kind)
4 ozs. of scarlet wool

But listen, it has to be
One damned fine negro
Hear?

* *Pacotille : As listed, the trifles necessary for the purchase of a developed cargo item in the European slave trade.*

Highlife in Blue

WORDLESSLY THEY faced the grim wall
Tested the pulse
Of the desire to live
By giving agony a voice

When they reached the end of a wail
They rested, if rest it was
And they questioned
The darkness that was all about them
With their silence
And the world of words was born

Then a slow bold voice found itself
Unrepentant, unspent, unto itself whole
Rose from the shards in the heart of the earth
Found in a phrase a flaming fantasy

Schnapps and Brass Bin

RAIN-PAINT rainbows
and with the same brush
whitewash
the castle

take him, my kin
send me when you can
a bottle and a bin
made of brass
(any other day
she'd have given me away
for next to nothing)
I don't take guns
or beads or gunpowder
The next village does

Scarification

THE SUN speaks to the blade in flashes:
Sword slashed the greening flesh
Maame held on
The gasp was not me
But the word touched the earth in me
Saturated wind with a howling
My hanging will would not let go

The startled blood fled
Earth sipped her fill

Maame chased fingers
Over the route of the knife
Her face shone
The scar is hers, all hers
Just as I am, too

In the hold

THE SHIPHOLD crept nearer, savoring the moan
Is there room in the hold for hope
Room enough in the pause?

The darkness rose
Fought the spirit within to a halt
To what do we measure the passage
From here... and then where?

The darkness rose
They sang the song before people began
Burst their cheeks
Filling the pause with fulgurating woe

They saw the stars dissolve in the water
The hold crept nearer
Equiano cried: There is a vulture
In my shadow, I am not ready for water
Give me back my heart and my hunter's shadow

Blood paused in its vein, unsure of the turning
Still the shiphold crept nearer, savoring the moan

Big Black and Ten

IN THE hold today
They interpret as love in the making
The gentle moans of the sea
In the arms of the land

Bought bold, sold nasty
Pressed in search of passion and gold
The impatient clouds sweep aside
The moon

Bring out the specimen
Big, black and ten
And give life to a forgotten surge

Tender with thrashing agonies
(Dark wretchedness), an unlucky creation
Bridges regret with careful loving

The sea gives breast to hope
Swinging echoes hanging in the wind
To avoid capture

Eclipse

NOTHING COULD be simpler:
History simplified as a castle
The wind stands mouthing
Nothing can be heard
Except the rainroar of the past

To hear the rain
Recount its story to the roof
Flash silver and sorrow

This history: a drop of amnesia
Widening in its pool
It hates to intrude, fears to offend
The past with the averted eyes
Is careful not to impose:
A gift of absence to the present

The weight of the braided days
A whirlwind coming home
The sun slowly blinded by the clouds

It was dark then, it is dark now
Give memory nothing
And it is darker still tomorrow

I can feel the sea gently rock our earth to sleep

At last we found the Sea

AT LAST we found the sea
Her cheeks full of laughter
She flirted with blue
Her skirt was filled with water
She spoke, and we heard
The divided tongue of lightning

She wore a skin of satisfying green
And above a navel wet with sex
And branded into her chest
Below a blazing legend
(Imported from Africa)
Was a ship of loaded decks
And it was weary with bleakest moan

Stand against the squinting run
I loaded my days in heaves deeper than surge
And the aims of night clasped about he sky

41

Meaning me and mine no good

COUNTING MY cowries at the world's edge
How much for how many of the damned?
Days of purposeful counting, vulture's cry
I am counting my tide sitting on the nest
And all I know night and day is that life is war

Counting my once upon a time once more
I forget how many went over the world
Went over the worst looking for the tribe's head
Above me the vultures hover in deep assembly
And all I ever remember if at all, is love is death

Counting my hidden blood in the deep under tow
All this blood, so much doubt meaning nothing:
Meaning me and mine no good
There are seasons of game chased in the brambles
And the heat is harder to bear nearer the heart
There is a weight and a blight on my chest
And all I know is that no good came to me from the west.

Cold is the deserted

COLD IS the deserted home
The large empty rooms
Sad sacked the sold empties
What am I doing
Worrying old graves?

Cold is the deserted home
The dead stretch of empty rooms
What am I doing, Ntiwaa
Trudging around house corners
Peering into empty rooms?

Kusi Appea of Adanse
Osei of Konongo
They came back:
I roam the compound
I am searching for those caught
Those who never came back.

Slave and Master

I BELIEVE in the sea, its prudence
The surging sea, the retreating shore
I embrace both, the exact virtue of water
The land reforming into its sand shell

Inured to need the land mute and grim gives in
And the abundant sea, warm with words
Restless, innocent and delicious as new love
Is wailing hump, still and still insistent settling scores.

The Dealer

WAITING A sale
He leans non-
Chalantly against
The garrison and the flag
And picks
With grey-haired teeth
The abandoned flesh

It is clear
He knows his place
By the easy way
His knees bend
The averted eyes
Under the castle's gaze

Guided Tour to Cape Coast Castle

THE ONE in the capital,
He pointed out with pride,
Seats the government.

It was the age of harmattan
Creak and rust
It was a scream, still is:
Centuries of shard when the soil
Lay in broken heaps as soil

This castle, he explained
Served as a prison in the war
Which war? I ventured
The Great War, he said over his shoulder
And the look he gave me
Said I should know better
We followed in a surge

What the Castle said

I AM at my edge endless like the sea
I cornered by sheer size an adventure of sorrows
And trussed the moaning uncle tom-tom;
I am bold with legend
I have conquered these gaping shores
With surprise laps of my race

I am my own sea, the jungled drop
I crowd the litanies and the laments
With vain blood;
I laugh at the animal cries women make
I am the necklace of long-irons they ear
The iron-collar crimson with suffering

I am at the very edge myself
I captured the land and its abundant blackness;
The number is fired and numberless
That perished under my watchful eyes;
With my pawns I checkmated the people
Whose resurrection has not yet found the key to life
The formula for counting the dead lies in my belly

I ruined the sea's virginity
When the evening dropped her skirts:
With such delicate arms and gestures
Did love reach me in my deepest dungeons
I am at edge a restless sea
Surinam Jamaica Alabama Nova Scotia
I echo the owl's surprise-eyes in the glare
The zombie-shuffle of four hundred years

47

I am surrounded by a colony of bending knees
A people made drunk by lethal fatality
I am the climax
The assay of thumping hearts
I sleep in the silence of scars

The silhouette of a defiled race leaps flaming
But its only a shadow
I remain strong in the darkness of my whiteness

white + black
interplay

the Dungeon

YOU GUESSED it
castle is a dream
Without windows

There are dogs, wet-eyed
Without owners

slave is as naked
s a peeled vein
a dream

The dust dies on the turrets
from thirst and tiredness

We buried dust inland
With anger and a voice
And a dozen brave words

full of sugary sap
and a national anthem
the young voices
salute their future with
"I am not worthy, Holy Lord"

There is a chill
And it is not over yet

49

Cape Coast Castle Today

I WAS green and in the shade
Days before my ripe mid-day
I was sixteen and in awe
Of all ambitions that stood in my way
Now in the dark sunset of my plea
I am freed from screeching youth and keen skin
I am thirty-two and in too deep to return
Here, then, is the hymn I must make
When I must deliver to my sole world
The call of aged youth and promise

PART II

PEOPLE IN ME

Connections

STILL I like to think
I am rich with kinsmen
Each birth calls me home
The dead turn a turn
Everywhere in my blood
Stranger, prodigal, warrior.
I greet all as friend and kin
Who have dissolved
Their names in my blood
And I, I look for myself
In their eyes

What happens when people forget?

WHAT HAPPENS when people forget
And what is forgotten descends
To the pit of the stomach
And the stomach rounds into a tomb
Womb of all pain?

Holding in the panic
Plaited containment
Damn the fear
By damning breath
Then, calm like the river's voice
When something evil has planted
A stone under her tongue

She gurgles, pacing the pain
Deep into gutters freshly insane
They were taken so far away
How are their ancestors ever to know why
Ever to find them without name
How to find them except by their cry?
What happens when people forget their people?

Second Wind

MY IDOLS are leashed
To my wishes
I return with no god
And fret for none

The grass pines
Under my feet
The night has no voice
To speak of

It is time to find
With the people
And take away the key
From sad songs

Cecil: Fly, Fly, Fly
(For Cecil Taylor)

SILENT CHORUS: the wind smiling ahead
Tell them, let them bring the calabash
The way speaks of seed and water
Yet the performers still look for harmony
They look for the seed of sense in water
In gaps that rage a sonic sheer:
"That shit" said the half voice "aint nothing".

Silent tongues on fire: form, expression
Passion by the fistful, total brewing luminous
The process is the magic. The process!
And then we stepped into a blur of sounds
No sheets here but a revelation, suns within
The fullness of intuition and invention
The melody of adventure, then the yell
A new wave of conflict and burnt resolution
That shit" said the far-away voice, "aint shit".

And the hands that never land flutter in flight
round enough to absent all senses
Cantata of minaret and chase;
O my Lord, what landscapes never seen
What you chose not to draw are here at last
Drawn and quartered blood of lynch mod
such gore, malice in the chalice:
fly, fly, fly, fly, fly, fly...

An Air *
(For Roberta, who sang crying in the dungeons)

I PITCH my ambition
No higher than recitation
My voice: go below and slow
Pay your way as you go

Let us reconstruct
The footprints of the voices
The last attempted break-out ,
From the dungeon-walls:

Here two braves slipped and fell
Wailing buried the silence and the centuries
Here Anokye planted his sword of war
Then unarmed and his innocence still whole
Went to chase down death
Over there in the crook
The chains bared their teeth
Then clamped them to over a reckless hell

Let us go with the waves
That never miss
An appointment, my voice

O be low and slow
Or be high like a bartizan
We have miles and miles to go
To find
There is no anger safe in the land

* *An Air : In 1971, Roberta Flack descended the closed mustiness of the dungeons and sang enough to cry.*

56

The castle is sound
Invisible in its whiteness
I pitch recall
No higher than recital
The ruthless devouring
No louder
Than the coughing footsteps
And the sound of seed going to seed

I rest my ambition, my voice
A simple air, my tune of choice

Tribute

SO I who have lost nothing
But my stylized tears
Found real Art, a Bird, some Roach
And Diz and dat bursting forth
In shimmering splendour
Voices of wondrous gifts and tales.
In the question mark of tenors
In the defiant thrust of the trumpets
In the glass-enclosure of tinkle-boom Bud
(Who chewed the ivory changes to shreds
Then escaped, his madness intact)
I found again arrival to restful triumph.
Hot Lips gave me the water of welcome.
Everyday and everynight we jam
Till the blues turn green
Then ripen into a mellow tone.
We gather with Prez, Beast and Bags
And shake hands with shimmying Shepp.
There's Pharoah who came in the last Trane
Cherry with his Fulani head, Mal and soulful eyes
Fatha whose coast to coast grin
Holds a tempest in waiting
Mr. Davis who must live more miles or die
Mr. Armstrong, the jester who is nobody's fool
Bessie and Billie and Nina and Miriam
We know Bechet, Fats, Marley and things ducal
We know the way home, that the Congo will be O.K.
And we know too the sound reasons why.

People in me
(After Abbey Lincoln)

WHO CALL me Africa
Must know me as gods know
That love is not love
Only as an idea
But is self given
In acts rooted in faith
To the voices of people in need
I am creator of epic wisdom
Retold in all people in the struggle

Who seek me must surrender
All they know
For I who was discovered
By the presumptuous
And auctioned by the unctuous
Must daily invent myself
To remain fruitful at the roots;
Now is earth's burden earthed
When I am as eternal as hope

I have given myself up
To the freedom
Of all enslaved people,
I am the refrain in the song of the gods
Song of freedom, song of justice
Even in extreme unction cross me not:
Who must touch me
Must first bow to people in me

Monk's Tale

HE PLAYED just enough to weigh
The measured tale his faithful way
From the solid stream
He dissolved it all into brilliancies
That tasked the false brotherhood
Of black and white keys
And nailed each note home
In the name of justice

He named it as it fell
In fellowship first of all
And in fairness most of all,
His Melodious Thunk
As he saw it as he called it
Thus he could shuffle, boil
And dance even in America

* *Monk's Tale : Thelonious Monk 1929 - 1982; aka Melodious Thunk,
composer and pianist.*

For Sankara, speaking for himself *

(LYING IN state, stateless
A body love has used
And reclaimed from the war
He is as open as the day
And as deft
Ready for every how
And old hopes born anew)

October 1983:
To remember, he said
Is to resist   •
But struggling along
For better or for worse
We pass through the storm
And emerge on the other side
With our heads high

The year announces itself
In spasms and perplexing example
But we hold our own
Through thick and thin
We are Earth coming up for air

We entered into commitments
Suggested, proposed and organized
We live or die holding down the line

We hold our own
Shoulder to shoulder, daring
To tell our truth
We pass through the storm
Our heads held high

*   *Thomas Sankara : 1949-1987; President of Burkina Faso. He argues
    that "to remember is to resist".*

My fetish for voices

I TOOK silver, the colour of queen mothers
But the king-maker laughed in my face
Fathers, they said, do not see any difference
To the moon all her daughters look alike
They have the same wonder, ponder the same glitter.
Blood, they whispered gently, has no memory at all
So go on, go on, they pushed.

Why Cape Coast, then? I asked.
Ah, they answered, their faces dark as old gold:
It is a puzzle still, the one-way streets
The wattle huts, the goats and cats
The dogs that warm their bellies on tarred roads
Waiting with drawn tongues for the flies to settle.

But, I pleaded, are there
No feelings in common
No far-away voices
Only old habits
And this store of tit-bits?

For that, answered the palest of the gods
Take silver, the colour of royalty,
And go to the castle;
Find your children in mourning motifs
And in gods carved fondly for the tourist trade
Listen for them in the throb of your running heart
The dust at your feet, the liana vines
The voices that draw us to the light:
Do you not know the world ends here
Right here, nowhere else but the sea?

Passage

I

The wind when tired
Settles in corners as dust:
Let it pass
Earth, sun and thunder in the flesh
All have gathered
Let them too pass

Let them pass
Their faces daubed with charcoal
Let them pass
White chalk, calico and yam
The earth opens to the salt in blood
Her hands are soft because of the rain

Why do you wait, O valour
When there is justice only in war?

II

Buy them salt, buy them pepper
With spirits buy them people, too
Listen: the world turns agape
Tide and blight flush far and deep
Call my mother call my father
Have they too passed?

O brave soil, turn, turn, turn:
It is death itself, the message of the horn!
The wind when exhausted
Settles in wild havens as dust
It is the people in prayer
Let them pass, I said let them go
Soil, heat, animal hope, bleeding fear
Goodbye to the sea, goodbye to the brass

Sunset, mirrors, colours miry and tangled
They have all passed not once but wise
Excepting memory let them all pass

And yet there's the pain

AND STILL there's the pain
The anguish of rotten green
But all that is hungry
Is watered by the same courage of green

The sea carries Africa on its back as an island   ·tempting
And murmurs an awesome wholeness
The passport to power, the source of all darkness

And yet there is the pain
Shall I behave like the sea
And throw myself on the mercy of the land   Sea is cruel,
Or squat forever like the sands   but quick, efficient
And relinquish all hope of an end?
My days and my nights breath in silence
The sleep of kings dissolved
As my mother carried me tumbling
Cover-cloth and pomp, nose stiff with ceremony

Anger crackling remorseless
Base cannibal teeth
Filed teeth filing down slaves
They will find these horrors too horrible
Run finger over old scars and shiver
The man with the stutter and the earth gasp
They will weep for him
And feel a mounting crisis in his vatic cry

Or failing that
Find ways to punish this poem

Equiano: A Mother's song

SOME CALYX must save my seed
And with living water replenish his earth
Something kind must throw back
The doors of distant laughter
Unbolt the locked land, and from timeless places
Across the sphereless distance
Call forth the songs of the daylight people
For darkness presses all about us, sightless
And tight is the nightmesh of plaited traps

They snared him like a beastly thing
Took him washed out in streams of fishy swarm
Scaled and sold him, my flute song
Where his mother can never reach him
My body is streaked with red clay
I will not be consoled

Castle Wall, wailing wall

TO SLAP the past with a name
To bring the story to its senses
To engage the living heat
To beat urgency out of the last gasp
The familiar confessing its blank secrets

Flake them for blood
For the walls are the dust of flesh

Report to Wonder

I SURRENDER myself
My fear and my weakness
To faultless memory

The jackal god
Whose breath drills holes in the sky
Turned the scarab aside
Heaved, and the sarcophagus, too, moved:
Precious oil fell as rain

I shall report to wonder
The simple fear today:
To look in the mirror
And find nobody there

Anubis: the face is the same
And same too is the name
The eyes of Horus people the sky
Cradles the city of the dead
The eye has six daughters
Each is a bride, each is a navel
In the horizon of the globe

I surrender myself to wonder
Faultless memory: punish the slave image!

The conquest of the gods

REVOLT LIES slit throated under the trees
And the dead leaves bleed into the wind

I have lived my life in slow motion
Negotiated bends and wrecks and a peculiar madness
But that is life under the sea

Reckless in the brine
Without fire in their balls
Among relics witless and final
Lie the keepers of all pain;
The cannons of the castle:
To think that these,
Rusted the colour of pithless blood,
Could topple the seven
And seventy gods of Cape Coast

I saw them hidden, the gods of clay,
At the bottom of centuries
These are not jealous deities;
Too tired, too bracken, too badly served
And fearful still of the cannon's boom
But that, too, is life under the sea

Seventy seven times blood

BLOOD ON the sun native and free
We live our death in open places
This is suicide blood faces
Blood pack on both ends of the ocean
Blood on the steps to the castle
There is nothing left to hide
We live this death in wide open spaces
And the ocean is encircled
All the blood ever drawn was drawn from me
Blood of my day blood of my night
Blood streaming down mountains
Melted blood seismic blood hot and putrid
Giant blood orgasmic blood
Blood of my blood hopping mad blood
There is fire in the blood fire in the sea
Blue bland blood blood in the bank
Blood on the castle blood on the rampants
Blood in the arms of the earth
Baby blood blue blood blood on my head
There is nothing left to hide
The stars are a field of flags proclaiming independence

Hallehuja blood cowhorn sucking blood
Inflamed blood newt's blood
The blood of the sun trickling into my beard
Blood on the sun natural and free
Blood of my blood true blood
O cultured blood polluted blood
Blood at high noon tainted blood
Blood at high noon rinsed blood
Blood money blood of the lamb

Blood of the saviour transformed by the serpent into hyssop
Behold the glory of blood rivers of blood

Soledad soledad blood in my eye
Gore all the shed blood turning to dust in the dust
Absent secret unbalanced blood
Blood of woe uncharted blood
Yesterday's blood invisible in rhythm
Dancing hearts frolicking in the rain
Nights with a taste for blood
O blood of my blood my own blood
There is nothing, nowhere else to hide

The Scavenger's rejection of grace

SHOULD I pretend then to such loss
As would lose me memory of my cross?

For God my God is lean and sudden
I have seen the slaver cross himself
And reason with faith in profit's favour
Against the blood, the wine and the lamb

It would make the restless sea still
To walk old devotions home

I go under fossils and things
Memories abandoned to shore
Scavenger, I patch as best I can
Thoughts nailed to the cross

Footnotes

I   DANK WATERS from which I drank
         To which I go, leaven of our slavery
         And up-ended myths:
         Standing in the rain
         Don't I wipe my sweat in vain?

II   Because I have nothing
         Because I have nothing
         I have every reason to stay alive
         Because I have noting
         I have a hold on death
         Because I have life
         Have I a grip also on life?

         In my hands, in my claws
         A gesture, a suicide note:
         Can I live my life over again?

III   I wish I could remember
         The faces of all memories
         Stray thoughts lost
         Between the lines
         Postscripts to my under-lived life
         In inverted commas I wish I could die
         So to

         Escape my soul's death in polythene bags
         Antiseptic shrouds, seeded rain
         An air-less death cheap at second-hand
         To escape being the tool of fools

IV   I have just come in, come
      From the rain into the cold, my people:
      Who knows which side of heaven
      Bread will fall from?

      And Oh, such malevolent air in the applause!

V   I go
      I go to prepare a place
      To open fresh graves, fresh
      Tribal scars one earth's blank face
      While angels scamper before my devil's rage

      Can I... but how
      Can I live my life over again
      When I have only just come in
      From the cold into the rain?

Against Fear

MY DAYS are full of veins
Where are the dead
My closely kept patch of night?
The gloat, the collapse, the glut of bodies
O there is no faith in the sea

Thus fear the touch of water
Simmering hot or indifferent to touch
Fear the eddies and the storm
The torrents and the calabash filled with tornadoes
Fear the wave that collapses around your feet
There is no faith in the sea
Where my bodies were last seen

Fear the chest and the veins, too
For they impact in reckless drive
The bold brown of rust and blood
Fear the slippery attention of charity
That slides within then heave scatterlings
And the dead stillness of the center
Fear, fear the days, fear the yearning and the yore
In slavering slanderous mouths
Fear the scars, the savaged innocence
The footprints of the wounded age on living faces
Fear the ancient call to forget
Fear too the fawning motive
And the sea that waves goodbye to the salt of the earth

Fear them all, the steaming and fuming out of turn
The dusk edging into night, resolve's folded arms
The cunning of snow, the future out of shape
The fashionable call to forget (O unfashionable distress!)

Or to remember but never enough
Fear them all, those who sing indifference
Who live and die with the sound of nod, indifferent
Fear lest your dawn changes its mind at night
And take you, vein to the sea, captive again

Six voicings

I   THE RAIN hanged itself from out windowsill
In a tiny droplet;
Nothing was left firm and strong save our will
Which must never forget

II   Death smiles along the mouths
Of those dying to war
But our earth that is hurt heals itself
By holding its breath
Testing the very edge of life

III   So much then for courage
The loveless who shout of love
And cowards and their talk of war;
Take that early morning
Which rose and walked into the sun,
And our days are a puzzle striding into place:
The world is without an enemy
Where mere desire is looking for a place to hang.

IV   As tragic as the death of magic
Living until rhythm rejects music
And there's nothing left but logic:
Religion, too, is calling on ourselves
For help

V   Dancing and dancing in the darkening gloom
The survivors carve their steps in the sand
Drums take command
And we are new markets in the boom

VI   I have bent down low
And felt the belly-glow
I have touched hoe on seed
O god let me live freed.

Confessions to Wonder

I HAVE wandered my shore
In uncertain memory
Balanced only as recrudescence
A winding twining worry;
I have witnessed the death of days and kin
Wandered uncertain in false accents
Inflected and fathered triplets
Dreaming in excess a catchy lack
So gross is the fear today
Yet take away the whining lament
Look behind all that has been said
And all we want is the Castle dead

The night's song belongs to the leaning hills
I shall report to wonder
On my way to the new kingdom
I shall report to wonder
The deepest fear today:
To look in the mirror
And find the Castle there

Watering the silence

THE ABSENCE is in me
The silence squats on my tongue
Even as I scratch the night for the light of day

Slowly the lights go away in the mind
And there is darkness behind my eyes
It is not sleep for it is not fertile or free
The air is filled with running cries
Of captives ready for the taking
Who yet find no fire to pick the bones
Or the words to free the mouth
Our silence dims the threats
But betrays the fear within
(The deepest wound in us)
Then leaves us husks in the rain
When thunder threatens:
What else can the disembodied do
When they cannot choose, do not count?

I will march through the sound of falling leaves
Through the lazy roll of harmattan
I will walk through the sands washed white by deception;
In my hour of darkness
I can hear the sun snoring behind my eyes
And I am kept surprised often
By the dead asking to live

We speak and speak
And even as we speak the silence grows
Watered by our lies

The clouds that fall as rain become the moss
And the moss becomes the Odum tree
Which in the night
Turns into the planks that board the captives:
Oh cumulus, how we love you,
Your root and your fruit

And shrieking and clamoring
In the heat-demented days
The captives march bent to the horse-whip days
Their stomachs swollen with silence
The womb of days ploughed through and through

Now at last face to face with memory:
But there is no mystery
The secrets are blunt, bare and worn.
Our bodies, bloodied then, are bloodied now
The sellers, fat then, are fatter still
And the buyers, then as now,
Fish down our throats to gut the fertile voice
They too swagger through the land
With the killing confidence of a plague

deprived of voice [handwritten annotation]

Can't it ever be known, or said
What passes between night and day
Between sodden lust and nullified flesh
When the light goes away in the mind
And memory waters the silence?

Nobody discovers himself alone

NOBODY DISCOVERS himself alone
In wicked places; we congregate
We party with wrinkling virility
Pretending escape, factory-fodder
From a closed state

And we curse every sunrise in jingle
In dislodged beats, a song and a cry;
Each must find an obsession in something stark
In sex, in chant or in a little lie

So much sorrow, longing faces pain-sawn
Gaping, silent, desperate; firm
Only in the anchorage of weekend rhythm: ·
Here are the desolate wilds of sound
And the shrinking will of every fugitive sigh

Our innocence, our faith, our days, our tasks
The laughing lying faces in simple song;
Something old left us here under the sky
Perhaps it does not matter
But can't we ever understand why
Nobody discovers himself alone?

Her story, too

A from oral tradition (handwritten annotation)

WE BURIED her between two illusions
Ama Afi, story-teller, last of the old
In one she marched with independence in '57
Holding the simplicity of my birth to her breasts
(Like the Bible she never learned to read)
Never to understand she was the past being reborn
A poem of hope passing for history

The sea is holy below her waist
The colour of her fire is desire in heat
Memory repeats itself to itself like a mad man
It is a castle full of blood money
This world turns too hard in my head
And when think I am here I am there

We buried her between two illusions, Ama Afi
In the other I awake to find longing for language
Knowledge of eye dissolved by day and sea
I go with care across the howling fissures
Hoping to cross the self-same water
I get lost in the forest of lifted arms
The clamour to cross is deep
And today, the bush is not the answer it once was

Exits

WHAT CAN I, Ama Afi's stuttering grandson
Whose spirit drinks in surfaces,
What can I save from oblivion?
There is no certainty, no redemption
The slaver's ship came bearing my cross
The ship berthed, dropped its code
And took on the promise of a new world

The cross taught us everything
Except how to lay its burden down

What can I say, except that they were here
Equiano's line, men and women crossed?
But the castle has sealed the land
The people are drawn in, like a hurt snail
The storm lies buried in the flesh
And they bleed wordlessly, hell in a dust-heap

Entrances

THE SPIRIT remembers how it felt

Well, I had my doubts
Stepping through the dungeon gate
But doubts are stepping stones to faith
I met the genius of shadows
The sea grinned, and those were pearls I saw

Why survive to make peace
With a life not weighted by memory?

And so I entered the darkness
Yes indeed, the spirit remembers:
I felt the thick blood roar
The walls, the must, the space all urged
But the floor was fair-minded
Smooth all over the beaten screams
It urged on the taste of blood

dungeon spirits

The spirit ripens wholly in the dark
Struggling for the light;
I saw no ghosts, but they judged me still
The corners jumped askance
I wasted temptation and jumped the dark
And I came down clutching my dream and drum

It's not safe to recall the skin's cry
The orgy of terror
The certainty of madness
Death's redemptive entrance
Hell in a dust-heap and peeling paint

PART III

FIRST TRIP TO SUNRISE

Theogony

THE STARS are eyes frantic with panic

Bathed in light
And painting the way
As she dreamt it
Earth soaked herself in sperm
Sleep lay next to her
Of the wish to kill
Only the shell remains:
The rest is lost

She rubbed together
Those breathless thighs
Out of both was born
Onyame also called Kwame:

The sun calls our turn
To the root of numbers:
Out of the octahedron, air
Out of the cube, Earth
Out of the world of numbers
An ancient fantasy borne aloft
Out of the world of numbers

Of the rest all is lost
Except the lean logic of the hopeful

Of Soil and Sages

A HEAVEN of stars and gold
Of natron and incense
God sits upon the moon
A tablet on his lap
And on his lips
A hymn of our new earth

He twitches and stirs the lewd moon
(What splendour in the offering)
Hymn of our new earth
Of soil and sages
And a tablet on his lap

He charged the eternal into being
The crocodile into the hawk
He is Ani, stronger
Than the master of the hour
Of flesh and the bones of magic

So let me receive back my heart
Lead me out of the dead land of the dead end
Take me where lush fondness grows

For I have tied my boat tot he shore
To the stories of goodwill
And my words are loaded with love and joy
O let me receive the balance
And receiving cord the taut time
As kept by the keeper of all water

Peace in water
Peace in the soil
Peace in the lake of fire
Serser, where stood the throne of all goodness
Peace is all who meet in the ninth hour
The ear of the ass
The knotted rope of power
Hear me, o love hear me
Soil, sage and hymn

Gesture

AND THEN one day, brave
At last from survival, I shall
Come waving panics last
Gesture at this wrecked world
And my innocence shall return intact

Like smoke that mounts the air
I bear only ashes
And yet unclaimed
I shall plant my feet among the ruins
To reap my souls riddled harvest
To straddle and survey the noble collapse of dreams
My future, my silence

By way of the grope

MEN ARE wild
And sure in divination
But men are simply men
In the hour of death
When resolve
Lowers its arms
And points downwards
A cooling yearning for revenge

Find her in the lonely vigil
The still winds of her night-cry
There is a kindling within
Of rupture and rage

I test my understanding
Stretching her flabby patience
To a tense past.
There is a hand, mine
Groping with her with staying wonder
She will not have a day pass a stranger

There is too much pain in the crush
Of living and dying in the midwife strain
The rain plucks familiar airs
From the storm's aimless forment
Of living and dying in arrant tyranny

In the final reckoning
Men remain men, women women
The child holds the promise
In hands that do now know why;
The questions that form, settle
Then escape as birds groping

We are the travelling country
(To Kweku, my son)

THERE IS a habit of energy
That never gives up the guest.
We live apart but will die
Tied together in each other's charge.
I did my choiceless part, lost a father
And just this last year became one

It does not matter any more
Neither the loss nor the scar of birth:
There is a song for every hope
And a curse for every imposing ruin.
My son is my history: does it matter
If it is too brief in my father's book?

We do not belong where we do not matter.
We left home and the comfort of our common clamour
When our fathers threw our house out of the window.
I was among the rush of harassed faces
(Blighted beauty) that double-crossed the Atlantic.
I have served my time
And yielded my youth abroad

We dream of miracles
But do not hear the call of the tribe
That know us by ancient names;
We dream of miracles
And wake up without deliverance;
The cold has frozen our voices
The wind sharpens its edge on our throats;
We are the same — exile, student
Worker, the classy and the classless —

We are the song (the day in fine sand)
When night grinds her teeth in sleep

There is a habit of energy that never rests.
The harmattan at our backs, pulp of rain,
How else can we live if we do not fall?
We are the travelling country
We carry our mountains between our legs
In many lands of restless cold

King Tut in America
(To Cheikh Anta Diop)

THEY MADE the good king pass
They bleached his skin
Cooked his hair
And thinned his lips
But after 3000 years
Who could turn his head?

In the night when no one was looking
They turned off the lights
Lifted his face
Fixed his nose
Cut his name in pieces
And sealed his lips
Then they charged the experts
To invent a new source for the Nile
Still they could not turn his head

I swear, I too saw King Tut
And even in profile
And beneath all that make-up
He was still smiling
After 3000 years he has not paled
So why should we?

Re-collection
(To Naana)

THINKING about you
I am absolved of all distances
The absences live again
But under the soles of my feet
I have no secrets
I have no intentions to speak of
I am unable to draw a curve
Where I am, resting at the last resort:
This is victory
Thinking about you

Homecoming *
(Report to Ama Ata)

THE DAYS passed the snow fell
I lost my voice a little hair
The days passed the snow fell
Death by silence: airless classmates
Sightless doctrines cretinous arguments
All drawn to their logical deaths, lush with ghosts

Desperate, I ate for comfort and company
The snow fell the days puddled
This side of dividing grey
In horror I watched young minds prime
To war an order on the grave face of death

And so it was, my people, so it was
Riveted, when in those days of lettered agony
In the distillation of logorrhea and cant
I found my form spine of steel
Bone on grin, silences' print on echo;
Memory became flesh

The snowed thawed with tropical glee

I raised my voice to explore the sky
From sun to sea I swore to weep no more
In angry flood I swept down gutters to sea
The horizon uncoiled rushing its length
From the arms of the sea
Whipped itself around my triumph and temple
And again and again the sky echoed my cry

---

*   *Homecoming : Ama Ata Aidoo, writer, teacher, friend.*

And somewhere within me in years gone and coming
The voice of fear grew faint and love very brash
A rushing calm gladder than the sea:
I am coming home I am coming home
Come morning, with the sun's brass and brilliance
I shall survive the sea's length, the sky's dissolving fist

Liquid days: O glory glory so much glory
My people my voice wisdom days
Let it grow, let it grow, let memory grow flesh

Judgement

THE PALM trees shrug
Their shoulders
Against the wind

And the sea. throws
Itself on the mercy
Of the shore

Who will judge
The captive edge
And say
To the land
Lost to its roots:
"Lean, my wind
Against the mercy of shore"?

Exile

COMING HOME, salt-in-wound faces
Down alleys of wild haven
Coming home lungs full
Of acid rain and snow
Full with too little hope;
Hunger for home is catching
Like a disease
When coming home comes to this

The keenness of my heart

WELL, THEY tried to shake an eager heart
But my beat remained acute
I could not hear the end
And yet at every stop found a new start
I carried my song up and down the street
All around town I played the keenness of my heart
And I never forgot those who forgot me.

First trip to Sunrise

I CAME here armed to the teeth with smiles
I, Kwadwo Okoto, Suppliant, Monday born
Son of Oboade, maker of every warming sign
Ah!, Odomankoma, architect of all human soul
You have not heard me yet
I am just warming my mouth

It is said that the farthest a man can go
Is come back home: labourer, mimic, hero
Here I am eager for peace this tethered Thursday
And they tell me I am the silenced majority
Monday, suppliance; Thursday, call for war
Friday, let all the wanderers come home
For, Sunday, and it is all over

Okoto, Preko, Akyin and Tanoba called Atakora
The seed is hard, heaven has receded
Our God and His majesty moved up against the pestle.
Today's elders dance the Apirede, but like children
Do not know when to stop
Obra! Obra! Abusua and Ntoro gather, gather
It's about us, it's about hour home
And it is about time!

They kill Piesie, kill Preko
They kill Sunsum, (they fixed the evil eye on us)
And still they kill

Ambushed as between Azania and Oguaa, Oguaa and Wa
O Tano, preserve us; keep us, keep us great Pra
Keep us seed in your husk

101

Husk within the amulet beneath your brass bed
Let the family grow in clusters, in clusters, in clusters.

This is my first trip to sunrise, the farthest destination
Take me, first born, to your innumerable self
The seed sunk deep; Odum, take root
Borebore, unleash the spirit of war
Then we can pray in peace here at home
Deep in the knowledge that
At the shrine of the foolish
The wise assume nothing but the need for scorn

Dancing with Dizzy or Manteca, by Mr. Birks

THESE DANCERS ARE NOT used to waiting for the beat
The music slides hot finders under their skin
And they step with the frenzy
The beat shakes them
The voice comes, collecting their wishes
And teaches them to rise saying:
This is not the time to surrender.

The singer leans her voice against his windpipe
Against pain not finished with us
His words cast shadows on the happy beat
He steps all over the chorus
And swallows a stanza in double time

And the dancers shake every step with glee
Men and women startled by their own bodies

These are songs to bring sight to the night
Make us understand night's necessity
Why nights are holy and full of flair
Even the blackest of all possibility
The night held quiet in one glass of beer;
There is heaven heaving to be born
Songs to command sleeping blood
And command it march forth
Gurgling like a last gasp
Songs to molest the dancing dead
Twinges and trills bent raw invading softness
And the trumpet crowds the floor
Slashes back and forth counting our loss
His cheeks in a dizzy bulge
He blows, clutching fire in his teeth

His faith is fluid and off known keys
Diz diz diz and dat...
Between tunes silence enough
To waken a sleeping river
And command it march forth
Singing like the flood.